THE ENCYCLOPEDIA OF GROOVE

BY BOBBY ROCK

Copyright © 1993 CPP/Belwin, Inc.
15800 N.W. 48th Avenue, Miami, FL 33014

Editor: Sandy Feldstein
Cover Art: Joann Carrera

BIO

From the international arena circuit, to his best selling video/book, "Metalmorphosis," Bobby Rock has established himself as one of the premier new performers and educators in drumming today.

Since studying at the prestigious Berklee College of Music in Boston with Ed Kaspik and Lenny Nelson, Bobby has recorded and toured with a variety of funk, fusion and metal bands; worked on various movie soundtracks, jingles and record dates; and did a three year, two album stint with ex-Kiss guitarist's "Vinnie Vincent Invasion."

Perhaps most widely recognized for his work with Geffen recording artists NELSON, their multi-platinum debut album yielded four Top 10 hits, warranting extensive road work and numerous television appearances.

More recently, Bobby has been actively pursuing a solo career as he continues to record and tour with his own band. In addition, his dedication to education and his desire to inspire young musicians, has led to this new book and audio package which is destined to become a classic in the field of contemporary percussion instruction publications. He remains one of the most active clinicians in the business where his innovative "melting pot" method of drumming is showcased for drummers of all styles.

A strict vegetarian and advocate of drug-free living, Bobby remains dedicated to his healthy lifestyle and regime of bodybuilding – just two of the many factors which play such an integral role in the hard-hitting, highly adept style of Bobby Rock.

Bobby would like to acknowledge the great musicians who performed on the audio tracks. Carl "The Fox" Carter – bass, Brett Garsed – guitar, T.J. Helmerich – guitar, Lance Jaxon – keyboards and Kenny Cobarrubias – congas.

Engineered by David J. Holman

TABLE OF CONTENTS

INTRODUCTION 4

BASIC READING 6

KEY 8

SECTION I: DEVELOPING THE GROOVE VOCABULARY 9

    PART A: BASIC COMPONENTS 9

        1.   Review I
            a) One-bar Grooves 13
            b) Two-bar Grooves 14

        2.   Hi-hat Variations I 15

        3.   Step-by-Step Patterns I 17

    PART B: INTERMEDIATE COMPONENTS 19

        1.   Review II
            a) One-bar Grooves 22
            b) Two-bar Grooves 23

        2.   Hi-hat Variations II 24

        3.   Step-by-Step Patterns II 26

    PART C: ADVANCED COMPONENTS 28

        1.   Review III
            a) One-bar Grooves 31
            b) Two-bar Grooves 32

        2.   Hi-hat Variations III 33

        3.   Step-by-Step Patterns III 35

        4.   Five-Phase Step-by-Step Patterns 36

    PART D: PUTTING IT ALL TOGETHER 38

        1.   Four-bar Grooves 38

        2.   Eight-bar Grooves 40

    PART E: INCORPORATING THE RIDE CYMBAL 42

SECTION II: FILLS 43

    PART A: TWO-BEAT FILLS 43

    PART B: ONE-BAR FILLS 45

SECTION III: THE RIFF WORKSHOP 47

INTRODUCTION

GROOVIN' - \'GRU-VEN\ vb 1. Playing with incredible feel and unmistakable attitude. 2. Laying down a wicked pocket. 3. Performing a particular drumming pattern or passage in the manner of Jeff Porcaro, Steve Gadd, Bernard Purdie, etc.

Whether you play rock, funk, top 40, jazz or country, have a lot of technique or not, or play at the local bar or local arena, groovin' should be of the utmost importance to you. The drummers' primary function, (as I'm sure we have all been reminded of at one time or another!) is keeping time, which is just a fancy way of saying, "Groovin'."

Now, in addition to the more intangible aspects of the groove, there are certainly some technical considerations for us to think about. You may have a great sense of time and an uncanny ability to groove, but if you're limited technically, it won't mean much as you stumble through a pattern that's beyond your present capabilities. It's with this thought in mind that this book was written.

Mathematically speaking, there is a finite but vast number of rhythmic combinations and variations that can be used to create a variety of different grooves. However, not all of these ideas are useful to us. That's why I have attempted to "trim away the fat" and present only the most practical examples. Learn a groove today; use it at the gig tonight.

Dealing primarily with the dense idioms of rock and funk, this material should broaden your groove vocabulary immensely. The majority of the book is a progressive presentation of all of the hip variations of all of the available groove components. This is followed by an abbreviated but highly effective section on fills. Then to tie it all together, we have The Riff Workshop: A collection of 10 different groove ideas and a "music minus one" audio format for you to utilize some of the material in an actual "playing" situation.

In addition to providing you with the above-mentioned tunes, the accompanying recording will also serve as a useful tool in familiarizing you with specific interpretations of this material.

And remember, it's all just black dots, stems, and x's on white paper until you make these ideas mean something, so: Make 'em smooth, make 'em "speak," and above all else —
    MAKE 'EM GROOVE!

Enjoy,

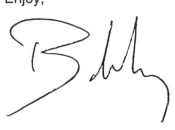

* EXAMPLES PERFORMED ON THE AUDIO

Section of Book	CD Track	Cassette (enter your own Counter #)	Section of Book	CD Track	Cassette (enter your own Counter #)
Introduction	1	_____	p. 33 (Exercises 1 & 4); p. 34 (Exercise 24)	37	_____
p. 9 (Exercises 1-3, 6, Ex. A & B, 7)	2	_____	p. 35 (Exercises 1a, 1b, 1c)	38	_____
p. 10 (Ex. C & D, Exercises 3, 7, 10)	3	_____	p. 35 (Exercise 1d); p. 36 (Exercises 1a & 1b)	39	_____
p. 11 (Ex. E & F)	4	_____	p. 36 (Exercise 1c, 1d &1e)	40	_____
p. 11 (Exercises 6 & 7)	5	_____	p. 37 (Exercises 4a & 4b)	41	_____
p. 11 (Exercise 9)	6	_____	p. 37 (Exercise 4c)	42	_____
p. 12 (Ex. G & H, Exercises 3 & 6); p. 13 (Exercises 3 & 10)	7	_____ _____	p. 37 (Exercise 4d)	43	_____
p. 14 (Exercise 6)	8	_____	p. 37 (Exercise 4e)	44	_____
p. 15 (Exercises 1 & 3); p. 16 (Exercise 20)	9	_____ _____	p. 38 (Exercise 1); p. 39 (Exercise 6)	45	_____
p. 17 (Exercises 1a, 1b, 1c)	10	_____	p. 40 (Exercise 1)	46	_____
p. 17 (Exercise 1d)	11	_____	p. 41 (Exercise 3)	47	_____
p. 18 (Exercises 5a, 5b, 5c, 5d)	12	_____	p. 42 (Ex. A)	48	_____
p. 19 (Ex. I & J, Exercises 2 & 7)	13	_____	p. 42 (Ex. B)	49	_____
p. 20 (Ex. K & L)	14	_____	p. 43 (Groove Formula, Exercise 1 & 12)	50	_____
p. 20 (Exercise 3)	15	_____	p. 44 (Exercise 21)	51	_____
p. 20 (Exercise 7); p. 21 (Ex. M, N & O, Exercise 2)	16	_____	p. 44 (Exercise 25)	52	_____
p. 21 (Ex. P, Exercise 7)	17	_____	p. 44 (Exercise 29)	53	_____
p. 22 (Exercise 2)	18	_____	p. 44 (Exercise 32)	54	_____
p. 22 (Exercise 9)	19	_____	p. 45 (Groove Formula, Exercise 1)	55	_____
p. 23 (Exercise 6)	20	_____	p. 45 (Exercise 5)	56	_____
p. 24 (Exercises 1 & 8)	21	_____	p. 45 (Exercise 10); p. 46 (Exercise 13)	57	_____
p. 25 (Exercise 24)	22	_____	p. 46 (Exercise 19)	58	_____
p. 26 (Exercises 1a, 1b, 1c, 1d)	23	_____	p. 46 (Exercise 24)	59	_____
p. 27 (Exercises 6a, 6b, 6c)	24	_____	p. 46 (Exercise 27)	60	_____
p. 27 (Exercise 6d)	25	_____	p. 46 (Exercise 28)	61	_____
p. 28 (Ex. Q)	26	_____	Riff #1	62	_____
p. 28 (Ex. R)	27	_____	Riff #2	63	_____
p. 28 (Exercise 1)	28	_____	Riff #3	64	_____
p. 28 (Ex. S & T)	29	_____	Riff #4	65	_____
p. 29 (Exercise 1, Ex. U & V)	30	_____	Riff #5	66	_____
p. 29 (Exercise 5, Ex. W & X)	31	_____	Riff #6	67	_____
p. 30 (Exercise 1)	32	_____	Riff #7	68	_____
p. 30 (Ex. Y & Z)	33	_____	Riff #8	69	_____
p. 30 (Exercise 4)	34	_____	Riff #9	70	_____
p. 30 (Exercise 7)	35	_____	Riff #10	71	_____
p. 31 (Exercises 3 & 8); p. 32 (Exercise 5)	36	_____			

BASIC READING

The following is a "crash course" on how to read music, specifically where the drum set is concerned.

Music is broken down into a series of smaller blocks of time called *measures.* The actual duration of each measure or *bar,* is determined by the *time signature* of the music. For example, most music, and every example in this book, is in what we call 4/4 time. This means:

4 = there are 4 beats per measure
4 = the "quarter note" represents one beat

Let's look at a typical example of 4/4 time in this simple, single-line, one-bar rhythm:

The notes used in this example are the above-mentioned quarter notes. (The numbers underneath them have been included here to represent each of the four beats in the measure.) The vertical lines on either side of this structure denote the boundaries of the measure. These are called *bar lines.* To actually play this example on, let's say the snare drum, you would simply strike the drum one time per each beat.

Now let's scope out some other types of notes:

These are called eighth notes. By themselves, they look like this: ♪ . But if there's two or more they are joined together by a beam as illustrated above. They are worth half a beat, so it takes two eighth notes to fill one beat. Notice that we've added an "&" between each of the numbers to aid in the counting of the eighth notes.

So just with these two different kinds of notes we can begin to assemble a handful of basic but useful grooves. Let's look at some specifics:

KEY

Music is presented on a *staff*. The common, universally accepted staff for all musical instruments consists of 5 horizontal lines. But since the drums aren't really a musical instrument... just kidding!!! Since the drums are such an entirely "different animal" than other instruments (in terms of concept and approach), we have more or less adopted our own "universally accepted" means of presenting drum music. Comparatively unorthodox and oftentimes varying to some degree from drum method book to studio chart, here's the essence:

A) We have a three-line staff, each line as indicated, is designated a particular voice:

TOP LINE - hi-hat or ride cymbal
MIDDLE LINE - snare drum
BOTTOM LINE - bass drum

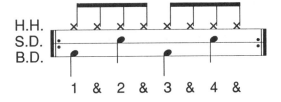

B) Hi-hat & cymbal notation is distinguished by the use of an x instead of the standard black note head. Other hi-hat notations include:

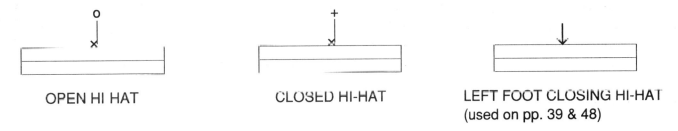

OPEN HI HAT   CLOSED HI-HAT   LEFT FOOT CLOSING HI-HAT
(used on pp. 39 & 48)

C) All tom-tom parts are written in their appropriate place between the lines and use a circled number instead of the black notehead. (see pg. 8 for details)

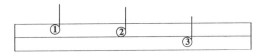

The second tom-tom is in the same place as the snare drum but is in a circle.

D) The double dots next to each bar line are called repeat signs. You'll see these throughout the book. (Technically, it means to repeat once, but you'll want to repeat each groove until you're completely comfortable with it.)

As you can see in the above-written example, we've got eighth notes on the hi-hat, and quarter notes divided evenly between the kick and snare. So to play it, one hand plays the hi-hat part, one hand plays the snare and, of course, the foot handles the bass drum.

In addition, here are a few other key elements to acknowledge:

1 E & A 2 E & A 3 E & A 4 E & A

There are sixteenth notes. By themselves, they look like this: ♪. Just like eighth notes, though, two or more are to be joined together by a beam. (Notice how sixteenth notes have two lines across the top.) Sixteenth notes are 1/2 the value of eighth notes so they fit four per beat. Check out how we count these.

RESTS

And finally, equally as important as the notes are the rests. Every note has its rest counterpart that shares the same duration. But instead of striking obviously, you "rest" for the appropriate amount of time. Here they are:

QUARTER REST = ξ EIGHTH REST = ⅞ SIXTEENTH REST = ⅞

Throughout the book, you will see these rests introduced along with all of the notes in various configurations. I'll refer to these as "figures," "rhythms," or "components." They will ultimately comprise the grooves you'll be playing, much like letters make words which make sentences. Got it?

We'll get into a few other reading-related concepts along the way, (e.g., dotted notes - page 10, triplets - pg. 44) but this should be enough to get us started...

Let's get on with it!

SECTION I: DEVELOPING THE GROOVE VOCABULARY

PART A: BASIC COMPONENTS

Let's start with some basic quarter note & eighth note patterns:

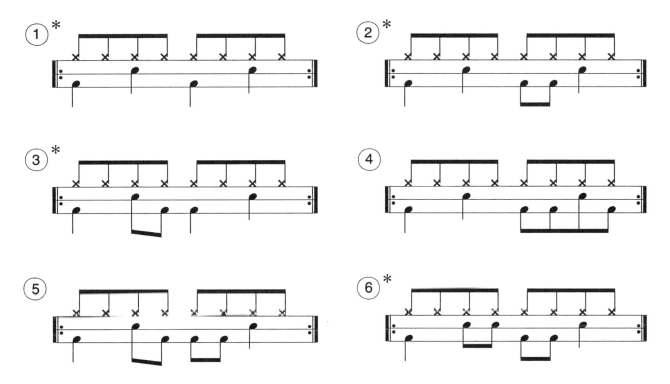

Now let's bring eighth note rests into the picture.

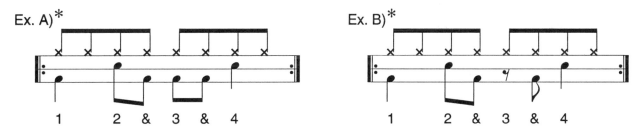

Example A is a carbon copy of #5. Then in Example B, we substitute an eighth note rest for the eighth note that was on beat #3. Notice how this creates a syncopated or "off-the-beat" feel. Here are some other possible usages:

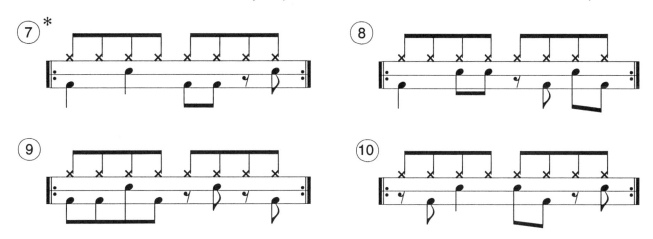

* denotes that this example is performed on the audio program

These patterns incorporate the dotted-eighth-sixteenth note rhythm. The dot increases the value of the eighth note by 1/2, which puts the sixteenth note right in between the eighth note hi-hat pattern:

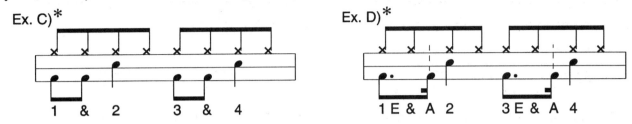

Example C is a standard eighth note kick pattern which, of course, lines up with the hi-hat part. Example D illustrates our new figure where the second bass drum falls in between the hi-hats. Here are some more ways to use this figure:

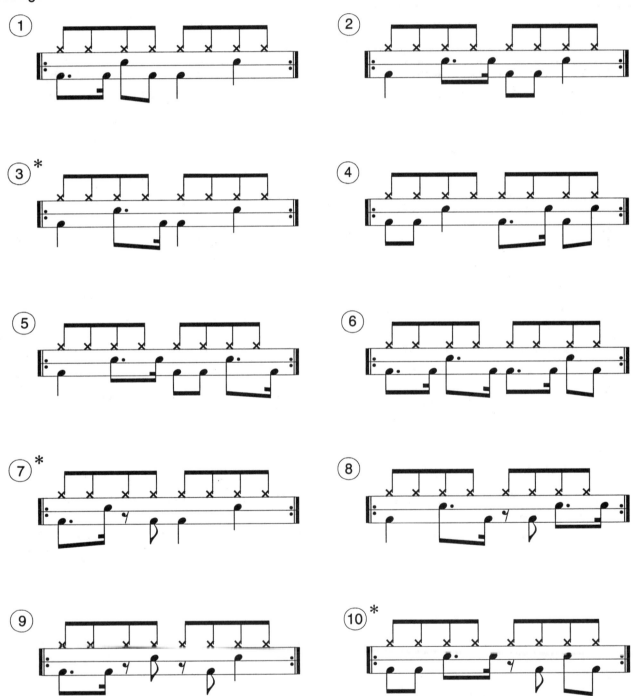

These grooves employ the eighth & two sixteenth notes rhythm:

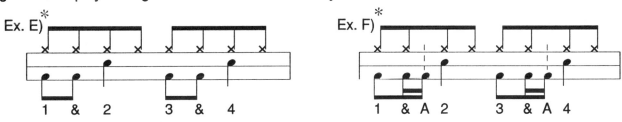

Example E is our standard groove. In Example F, you simply "double-up" on the second kick of each eighth note figure, thus creating two sixteenth notes in the space of one eighth note. The first sixteenth note still lines up with the hi-hat, while the second falls just after.

Here are all available interpretations of this figure:

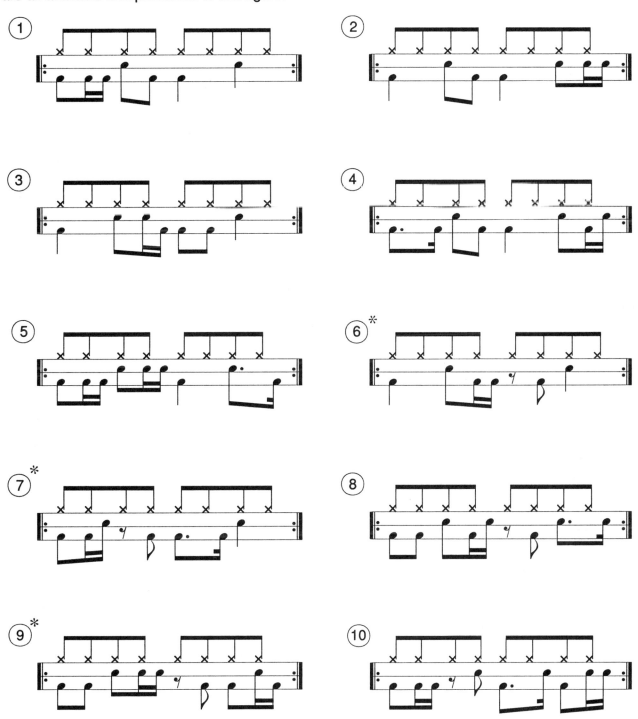

Here are some examples using the two sixteenth and eighth note rhythm:

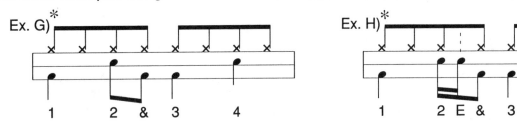

This new figure is actually the mirror image of the preceding one. In Example G, we have a regular groove with single snare hits. Then in example H, we "double up" on the snare on beat #2 by using sixteenth notes. Notice how the second snare drum falls in between the two hi-hat s.

Here are some other typical applications of this rhythm:

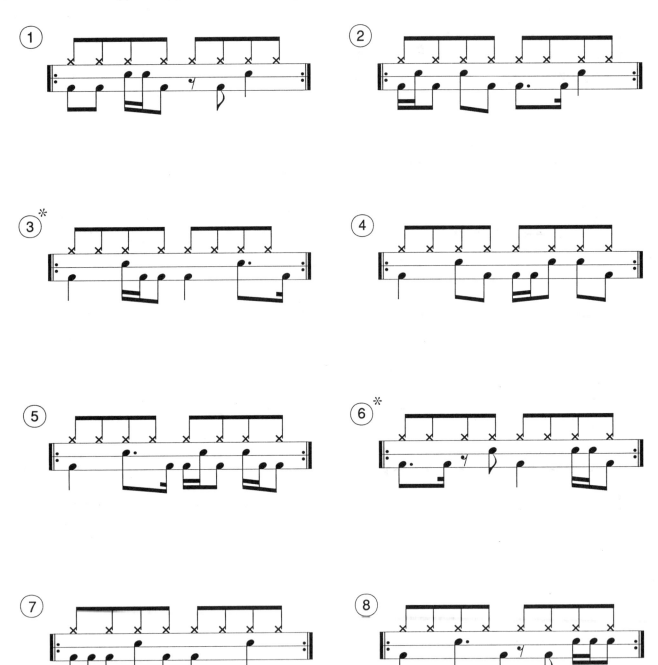

REVIEW I

One-bar Grooves

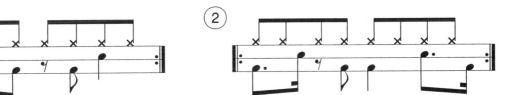

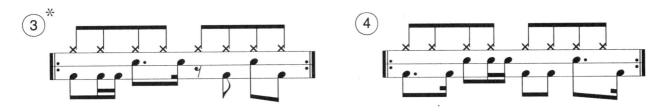

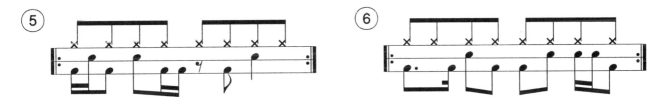

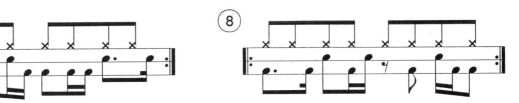

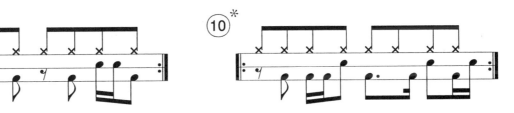

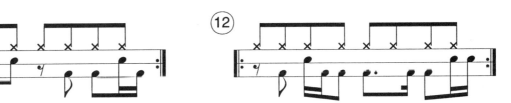

14

Two-bar Grooves

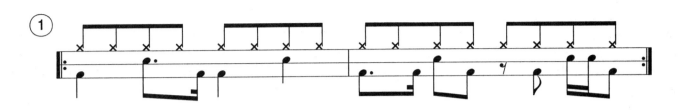

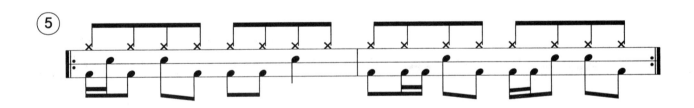

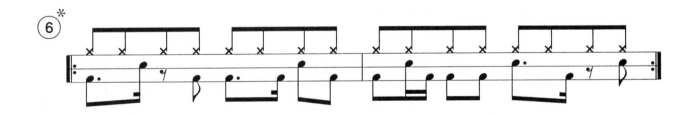

HI-HAT VARIATIONS I

A popular variation of the straight eighth note hi-hat concept is the use of hi-hat openings. As indicated in our key on page 8, you simply open the hats on the "o" symbol, then close them on the "+" symbol. This enables you to convey a separate rhythmic idea with the hi-hat while still maintaining a given kick/snare pattern. Check out these one-bar examples:

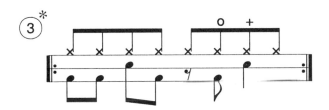

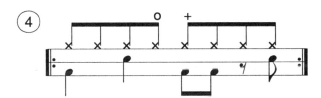

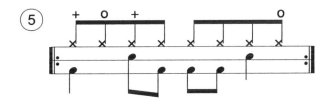

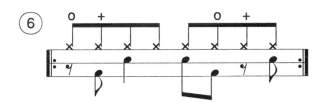

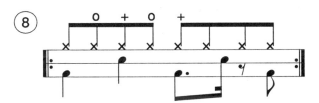

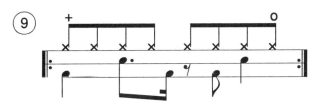

16

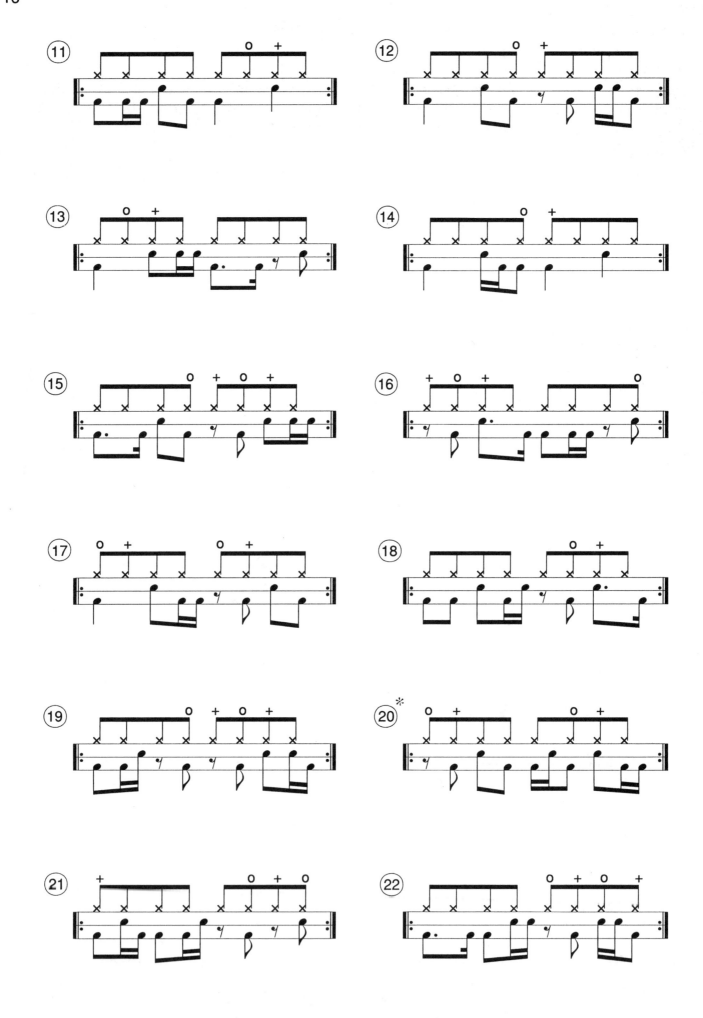

EL03821

STEP-BY-STEP PATTERNS I

As the name implies, these grooves are presented in four stages, with each one featuring a progressively more complex hi-hat part. Example A will always be straight eighths, with B, C & D introducing one of the one-beat rhythmic figures or open/closed hi-hat ideas that we've studied thus far. So as the kick and snare part remains constant throughout each cycle, this approach will enable you to gradually work up to the more difficult hi-hat part in Example D, while also exposing you to a variety of integrated hi-hat parts. Check it out:

1a)*
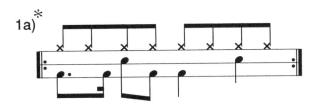

1b)*
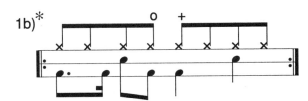

1c)*
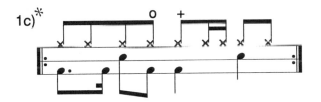

1d)*
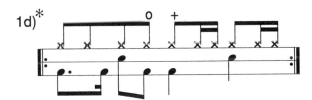

2a)

2b)

2c)

2d)

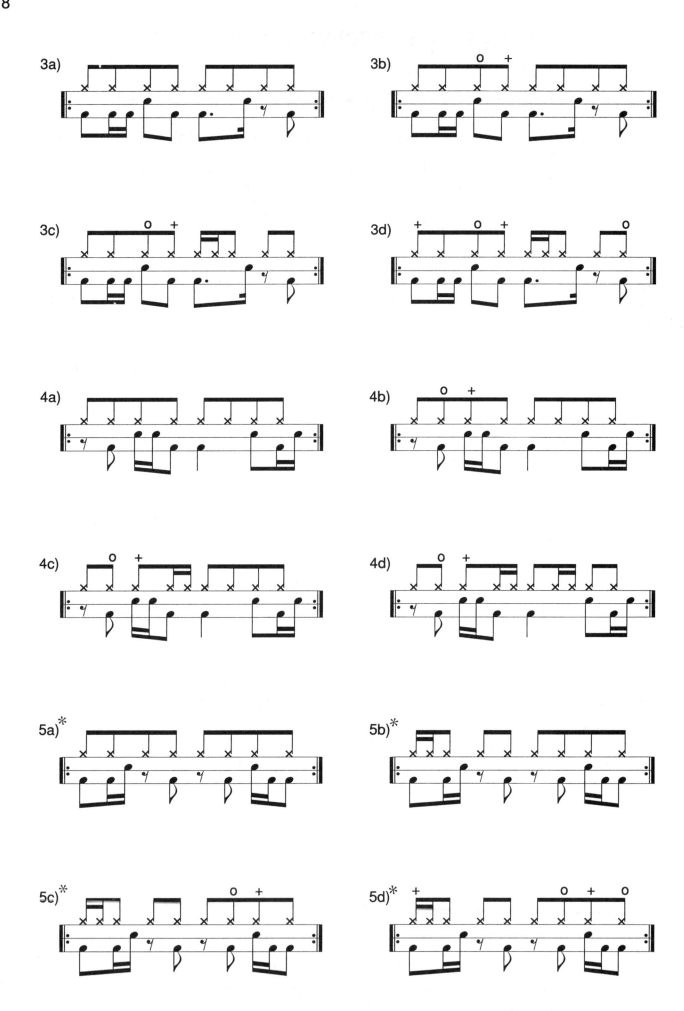

PART B: INTERMEDIATE COMPONENTS

Let's look at some one-beat components comprised entirely of sixteenth notes:

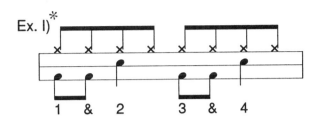

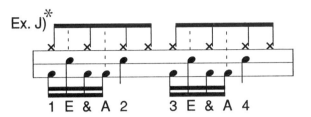

Remember Example I? I hope so! Now check out Example J. We've added a snare on the "e" and a bass drum on the "a" of beats #1 and 3. As indicated, these notes fall in between the hi-hat part. Here are some other sixteenth note components:

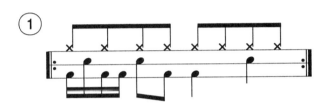

So far, most of the one-beat figures we've had have been predominately downbeat oriented. Now let's get into some more syncopated-based components.

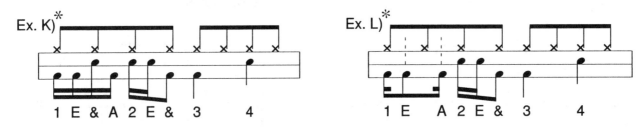

Example K is one of our preceding grooves featuring the "all sixteenth notes" components. Then on beat #1 in Example L, we create a new figure by removing the "and" of the beat, further emphasizing the "e" and the "a." Here are some grooves utilizing all of the possible variations of this new idea.

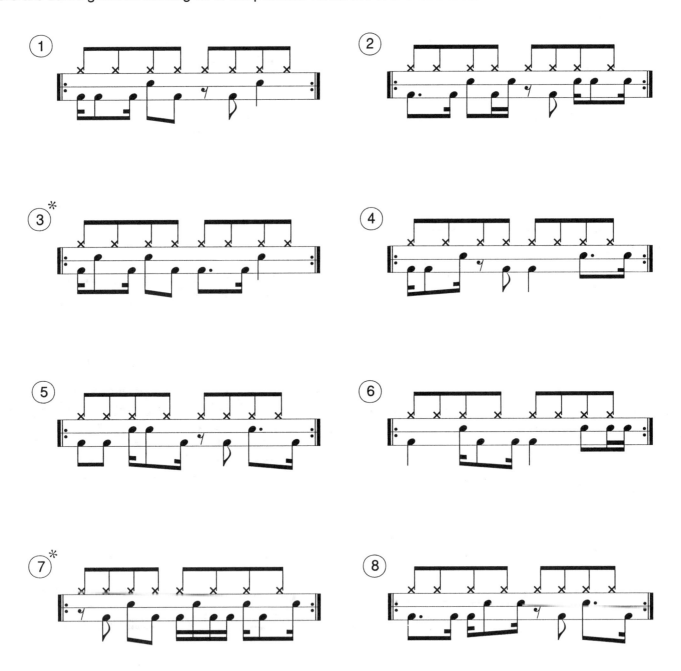

The following are various two note components:

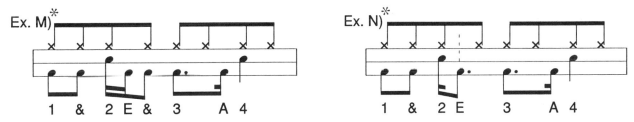

On beat #2 in Example M, we have our standard two sixteenths and an eighth note component. Then in Example N, we transform this figure by changing the second sixteenth note to a dotted eighth note, thereby prolonging its value. This also eliminates the eighth note on the "&" of two, further emphasizing the "e" of two. Here are all of the available combinations:

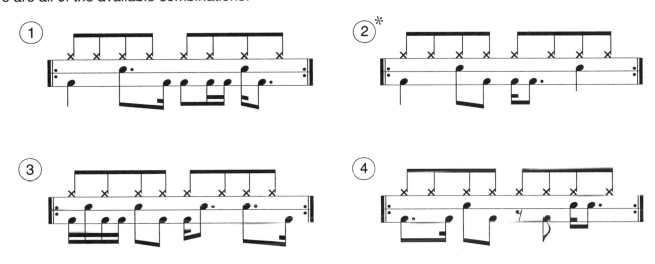

Here's a variation on the eighth and two sixteenths figure:

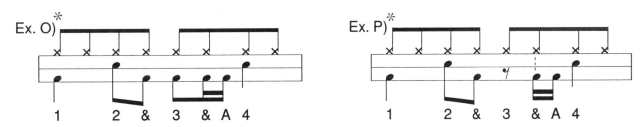

Example O is business as usual. Then in Example P, we simply substitute the eighth note on beat #3 with an eighth rest, which gives us yet another syncopated component. Here are all of the variations:

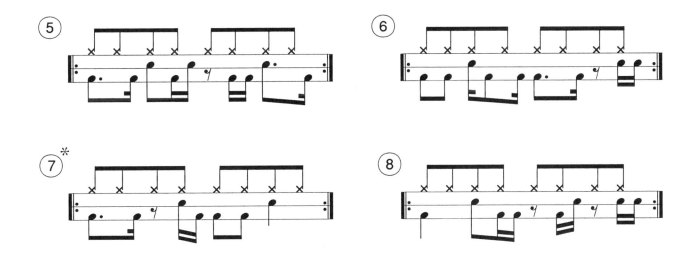

REVIEW II

One-bar Grooves

①

② *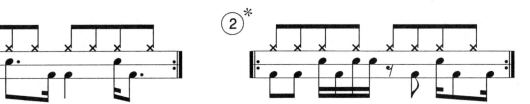

③

④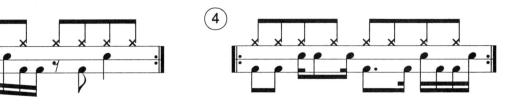

⑤

⑥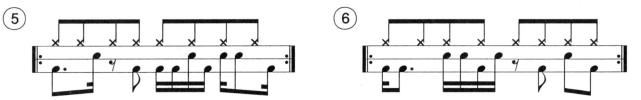

⑦

⑧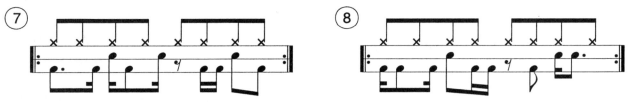

⑨ *

⑩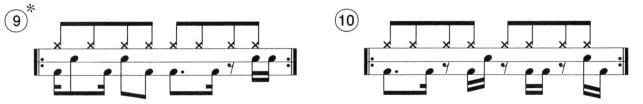

⑪

⑫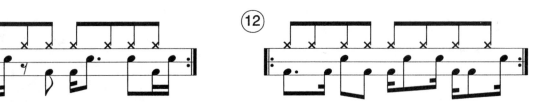

Two-bar Grooves

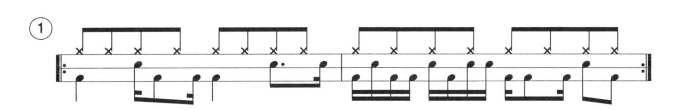

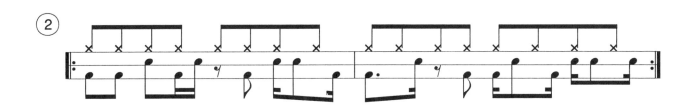

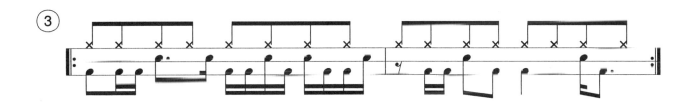

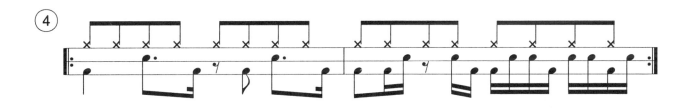

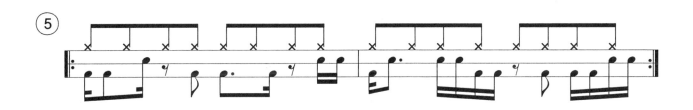

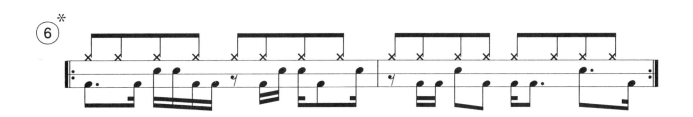

HI-HAT VARIATIONS II

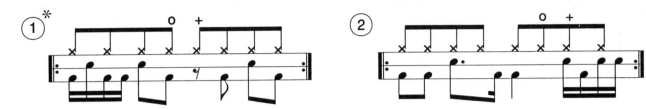

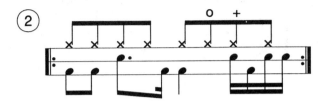

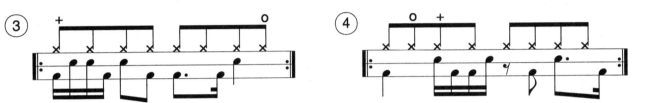

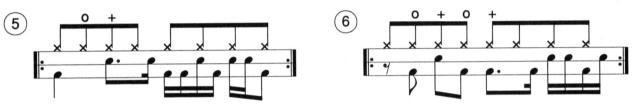

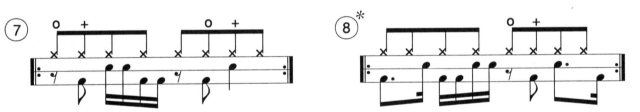

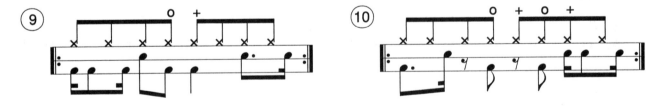

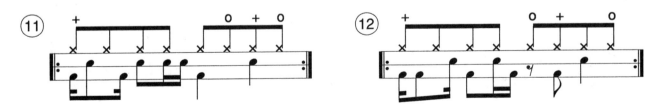

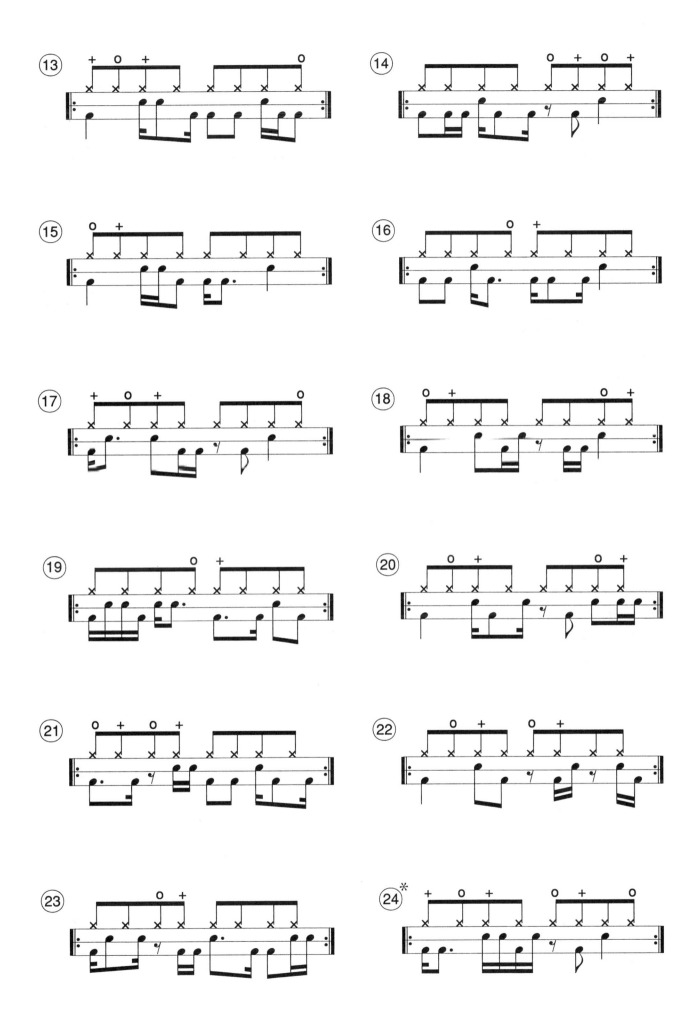

STEP-BY-STEP PATTERNS II

1a)*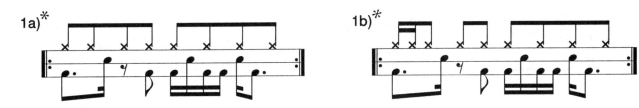

1b)*

1c)*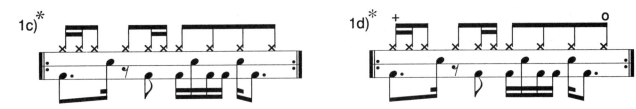

1d)*

2a)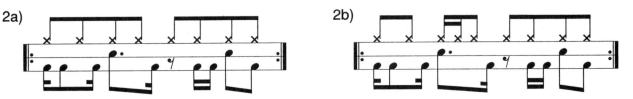

2b)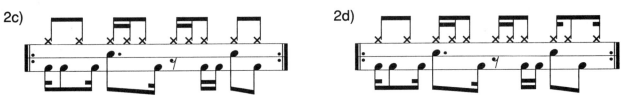

2c)

2d)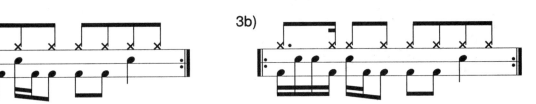

3a)

3b)

3c)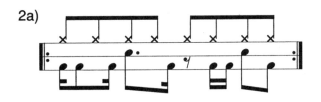

3d)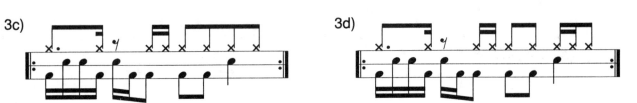

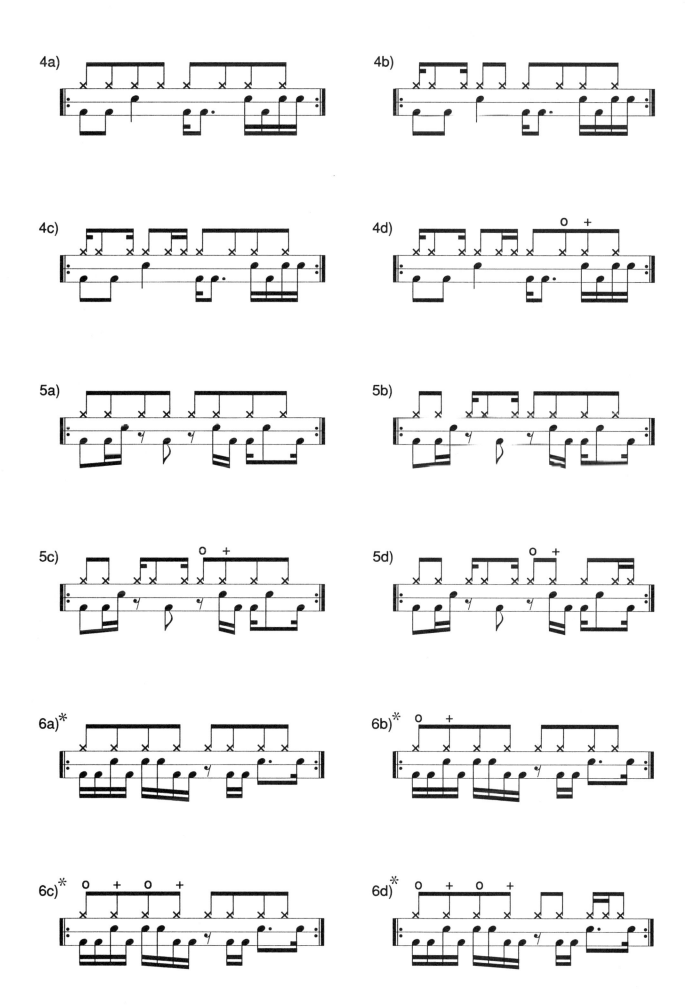

PART C: ADVANCED COMPONENTS

Here's a variation of the two sixteenth and an eighth note figure:

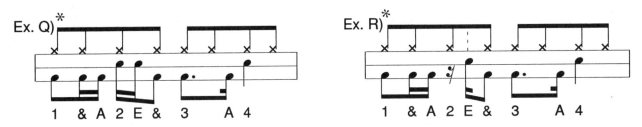

Example Q shows a standard usage of this figure on beat #2. Example R introduces a new component by substituting the first sixteenth note on beat #2 with a sixteenth note rest. Here are all four combinations:

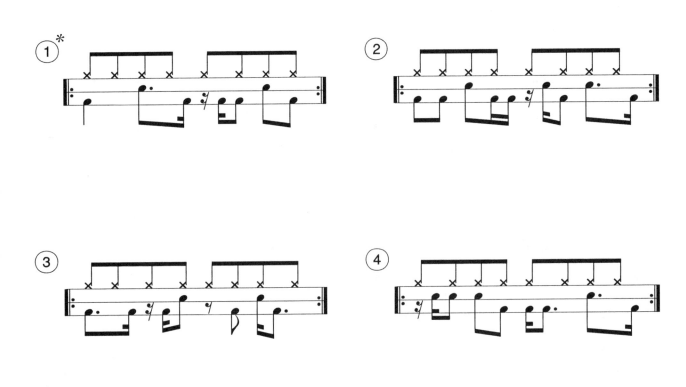

This last two-note component is super funky!

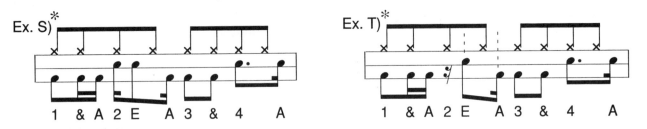

Beat #2 in Example S finds our good ol' sixteenth-eighth-sixteenth note figure back in action. Then in Example T we swap the first sixteenth note with a sixteenth note rest which gives us a new, heavily syncopated component that falls completely between the eighth note hi-hat part.

Here are all of the combinations:

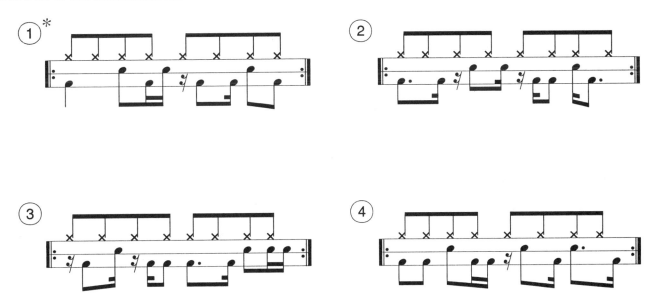

Now let's check out a couple of single-note components.

Example U and Example V

In Example U, we find a couple of the dotted-eighth-sixteenth note figures. Then in Example V on beat #2, we substitute the dotted-eighth note with a dotted-eighth rest which gives us a new component. There are obviously only two ways to play it.

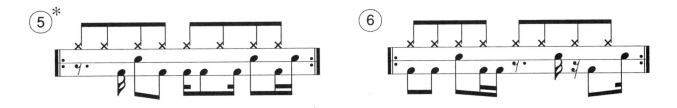

Our remaining single-note component involves a sixteenth note rest followed by a dotted eighth note.

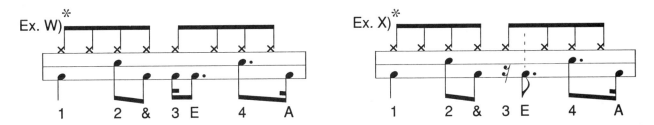

Example W shows our sixteenth and a dotted eighth note figure on beat #3, while Example X reveals a new component as we swap a sixteenth rest for the sixteenth note.

Here are the two available ways to play it:

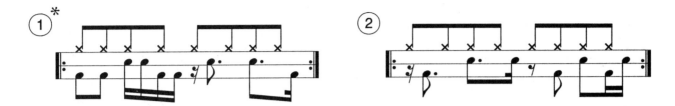

And finally, here's a component based from our "all sixteenth notes" figure.

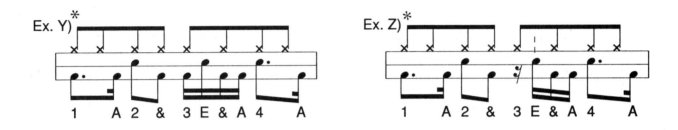

Check out the "sixteenth notes" figure on beat #3 in Example Y, then notice what happens when we add a sixteenth rest on the downbeat of 3 in Example Z; we create another component! Here are some patterns that showcase some of the most effective variations of this new figure.

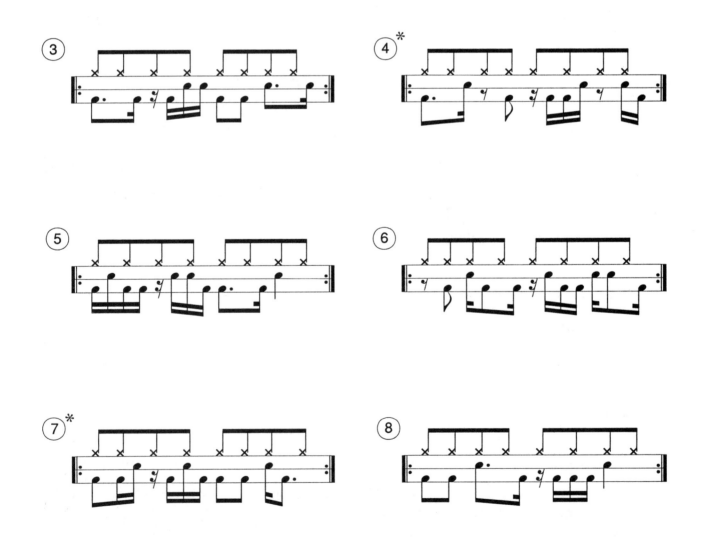

REVIEW III

One-bar Grooves

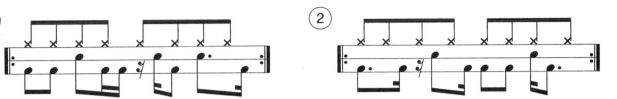

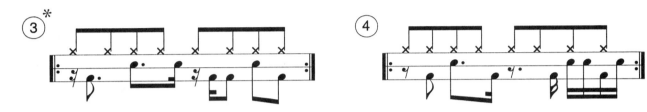

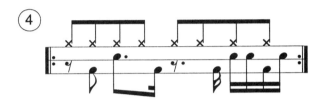

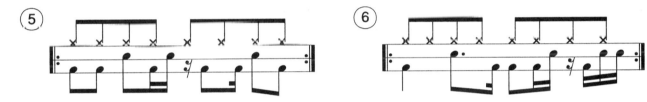

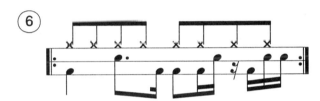

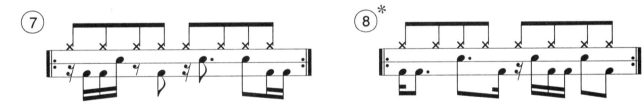

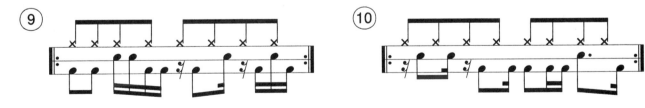

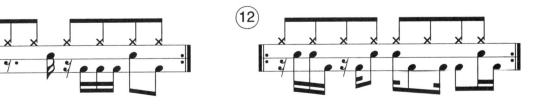

32

Two-bar Grooves

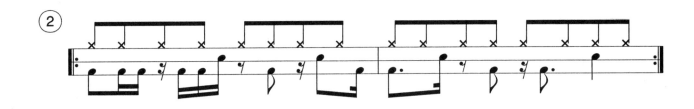

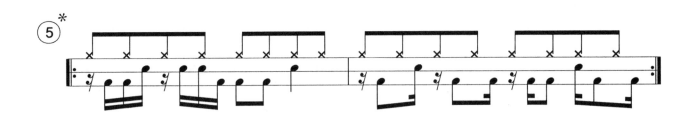

HI-HAT VARIATIONS III

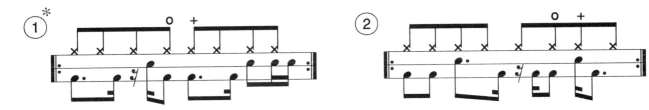

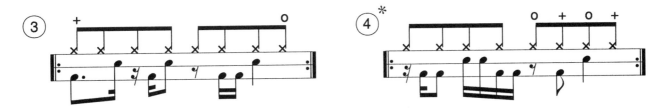

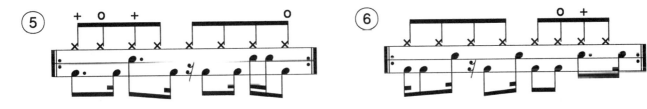

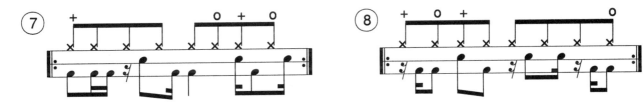

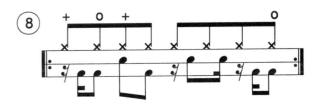

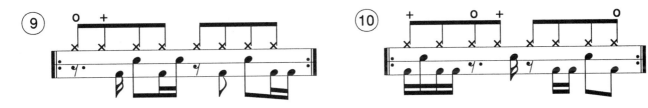

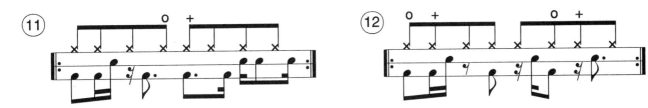

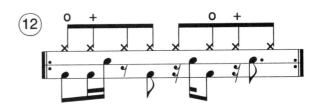

EL03821

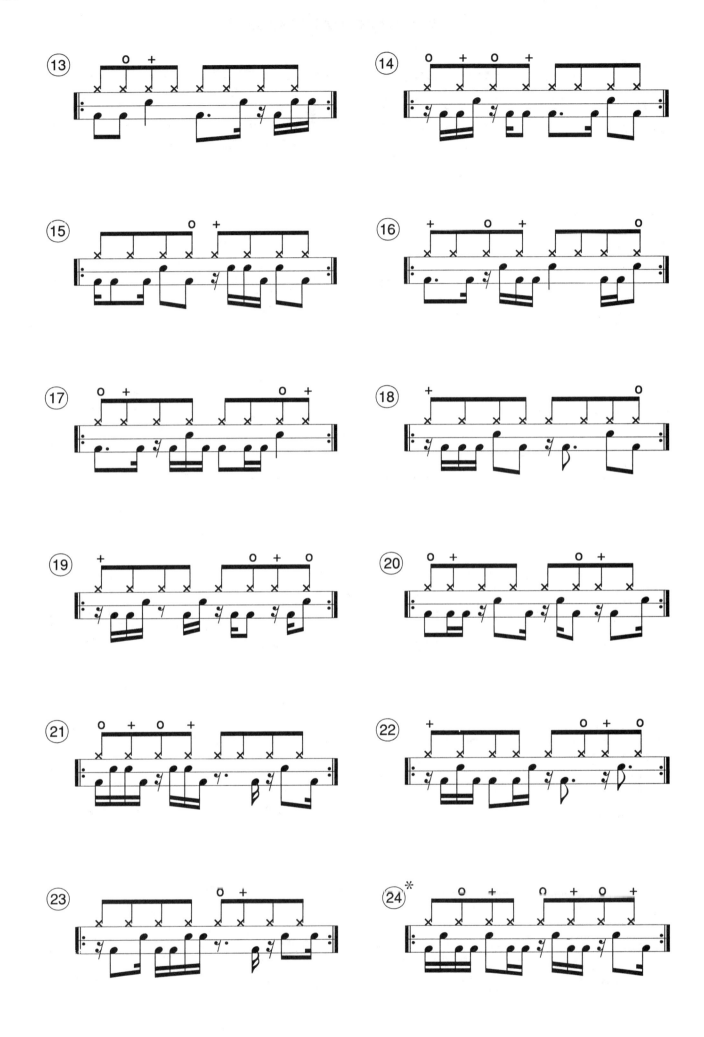

STEP-BY-STEP PATTERNS III

1a)*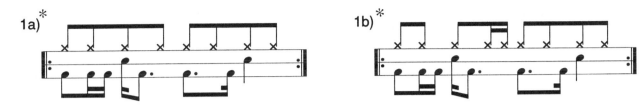

1b)*

1c)*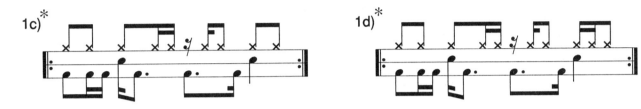

1d)*

2a)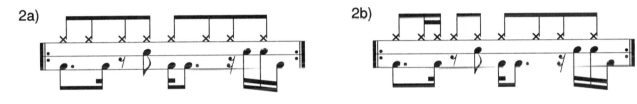

2b)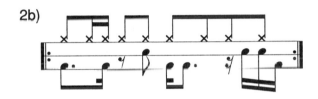

2c)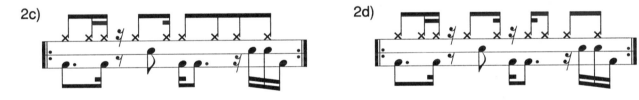

2d)

3a)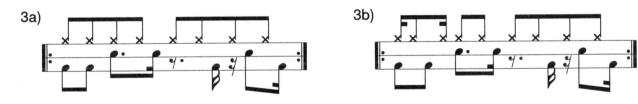

3b)

3c)

3d)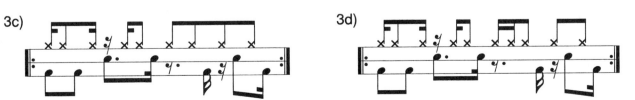

FIVE-PHASE STEP-BY-STEP PATTERNS

1a)*

1b)*

1c)*

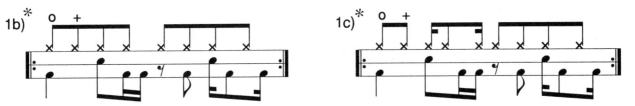

1d)*

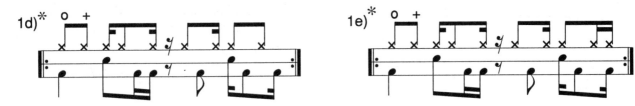

1e)*

2a)

2b)

2c)

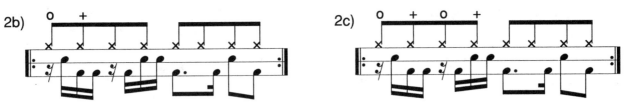

2d)

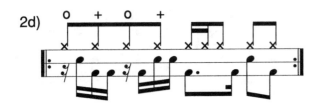

2e)

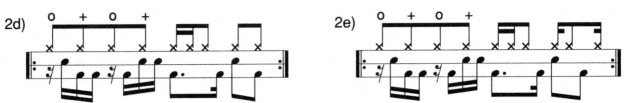

3a)

3b)

3c)

3d)

3e)

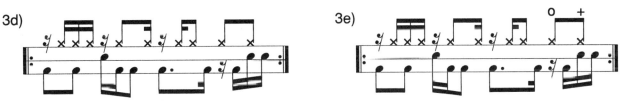

4a)*

4b)*

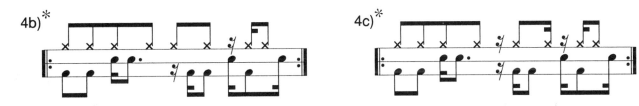

4c)*

4d)*

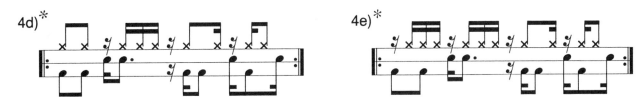

4e)*

PART D: PUTTING IT ALL TOGETHER

At this point, we've covered virtually every variation of all available one-beat components. Now let's look at a few different examples of integrating these components in longer musical phrases:

FOUR-BAR GROOVES

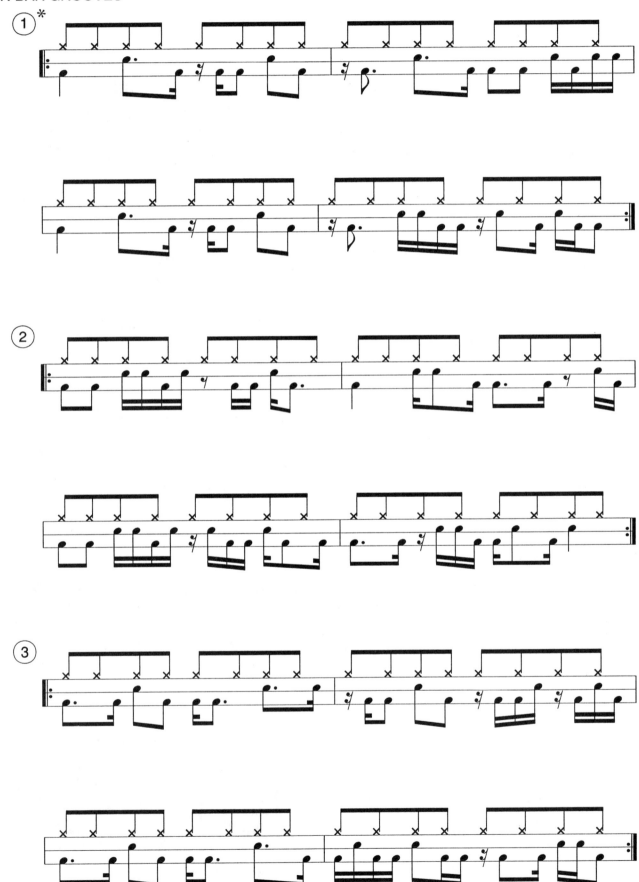

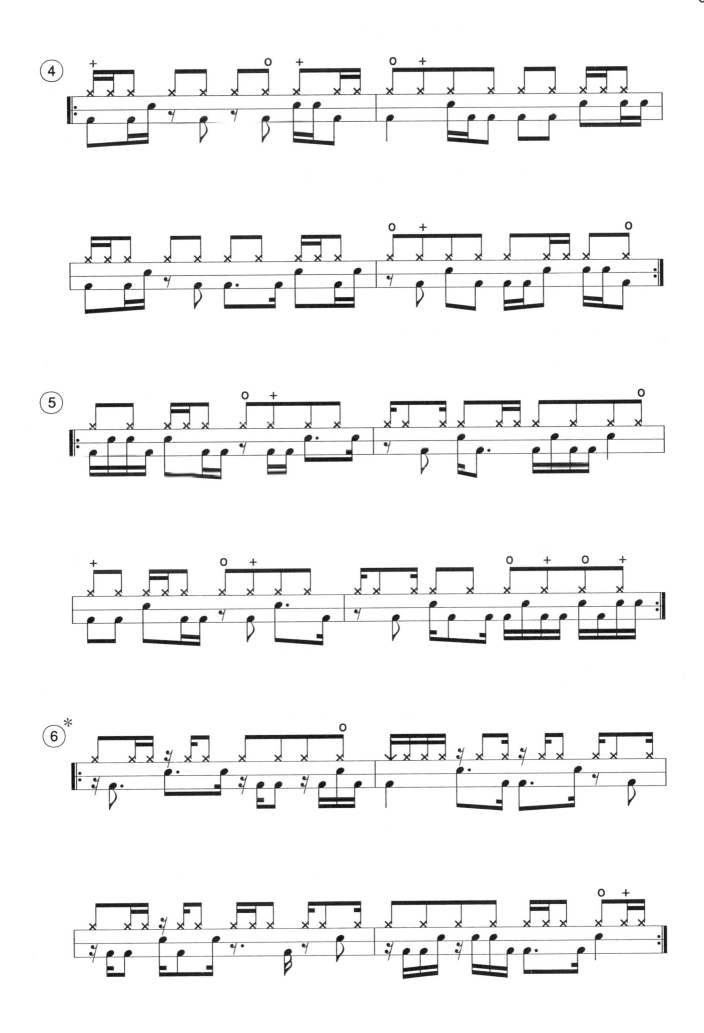

40

Eight-Bar Grooves

Here are some eight-bar examples. You might try practicing these one or two bars at a time before playing the entire pattern.

continued...

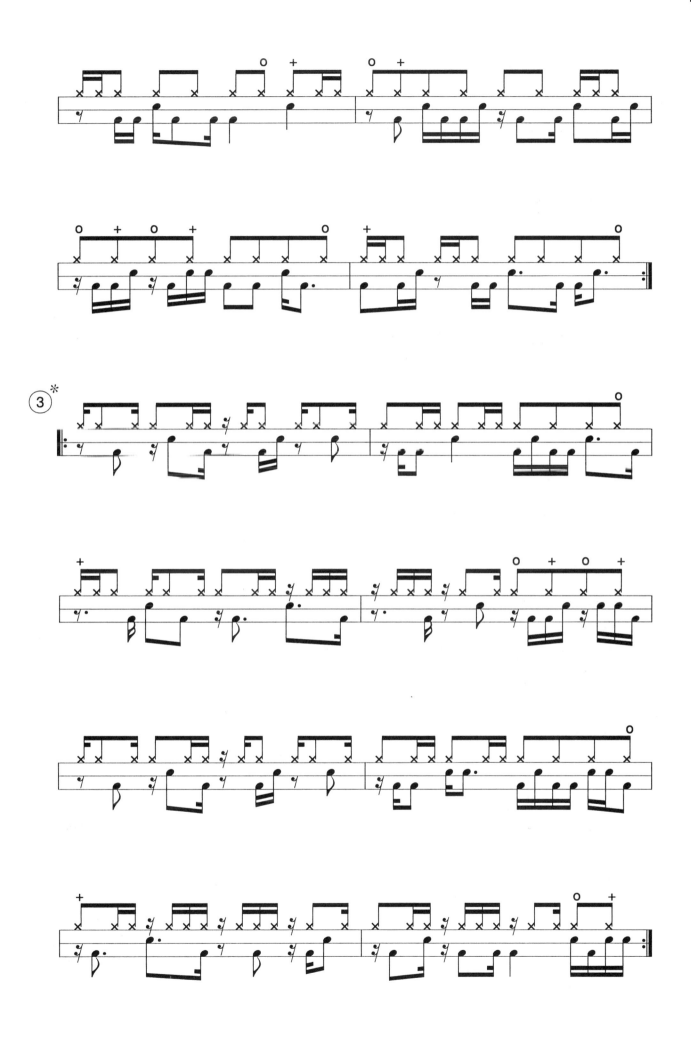

PART E: INCORPORATING THE RIDE CYMBAL

So far, all of the material that we've covered has dealt strictly with the hi-hat, bass drum and snare drum. This has enabled us to really focus on developing new levels of independence between the limbs as well as expand our rhythmic vocabulary.

Now let's look at a few different ways in which we might incorporate the ride cymbal within the context of the preceding material.

1) Simply perform all of the right hand hi-hat parts on the ride cymbal. (Obviously, ignore any open/closed hi-hat symbols.) Some examples will sound better than others, but at least you'll get a good idea about how different the patterns can sound by using the ride cymbal.

2) While initially you'll want to hit the flat part of the cymbal with the tip of the stick, you might try using the shoulder of the stick on the bell of the ride as yet another potential sound source. This is particularly effective when applied to the more complex, syncopated R.H. rhythms found in Parts C & D.

3) For the especially studious, how about stepping into the "Land of Four-way Independence?" With your right hand still on the ride cymbal, try playing either quarter notes or upbeat eighth notes with your left foot on the hi-hat. Here's what Example I on page 9 would look like:

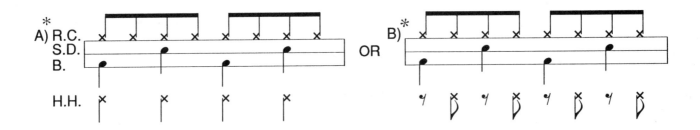

This four-way independence concept is, of course, another "can of beans" in itself that we'll explore more thoroughly in a later volume. But for now, try experimenting with one or both of these left foot hi-hat parts while groovin' with the ride cymbal.

Either way, I'm sure you'll find the integration of the ride cymbal to be a very essential part of your drumming arsenal, if it isn't already!

SECTION II: FILLS

Fills are generally one-line rhythmic statements that involve either one or several pieces of the drum set. They are used to signify the end of one musical phrase or part of a song and/or to set up the beginning of another. Ranging in duration anywhere from one-beat to many bars, we'll focus on the most prevalent examples: two-beat and one-bar fills.

PART A: TWO-BEAT FILLS

Here's a basic "groove formula" with which you can practice applying the following two-beat fill ideas:*

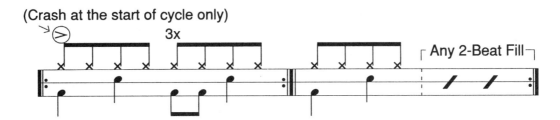

This particular pattern is just one of hundreds that you could feasibly use in this format. (Virtually any other one or two-bar groove found in this book could be utilized in this formula.) Now, simply incorporate each of the following fills in the appropriate place (second half of the 4th measure) to complete the phrase. After mastering each new fill individually, run the entire pattern down at least four times.

Let's start with some simple but effective snare/snare kick combinations:

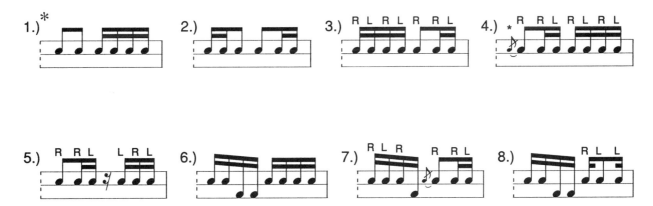

Now let's bring in the toms:

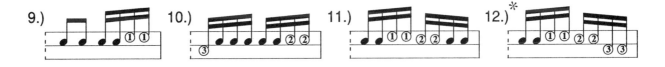

* A flam ♪ combines a softly executed "grace note" performed almost simultaneously with, but just prior to the main note. A flam creates a slightly elongated sound.

EL03821

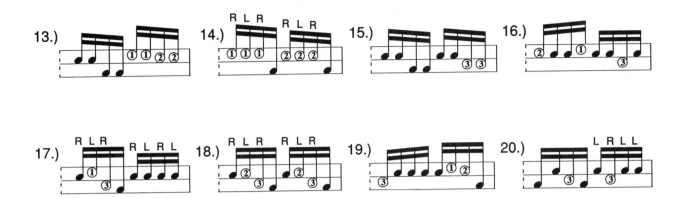

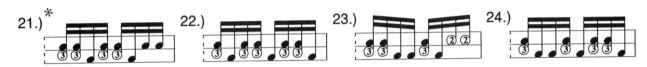

Here's some that involve hitting the snare and floor tom simultaneously:

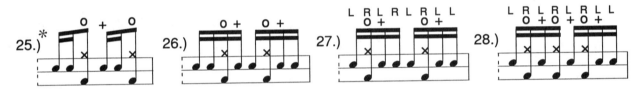

These fills incorporate the open/closed hi-hat concept:

Let's get into some sixteenth note triplet ideas:

Ex. A)   Ex. B)   Ex. C)   Ex. D)

Example A is our normal sixteenth note figure with two notes on the downbeat and two on the up, right? Then in Example B we have sixteenth note triplets which have three on the down and three on the up. (Notice how the number 6 and the brackets are used to differentiate these kinds of sixteenth notes from the "regular" kind.) Examples C & D likewise illustrate another kind of triplet evolution as Example C features two regular sixteenth notes on the downbeat, while Example D includes a triplet figure. Here are some 2-beat fills that involve these triplet ideas:

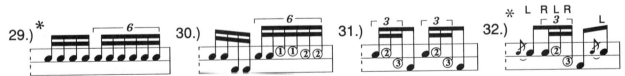

PART B: ONE-BAR FILLS

This section is set up like the preceding one. We'll have our groove formula laid out with the 4th bar left open for you to insert each of the following one-bar fill ideas:*

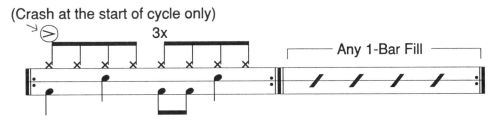

Once again, any one-bar pattern could be repeated three times before playing a fill to conform to this four-bar phrase.

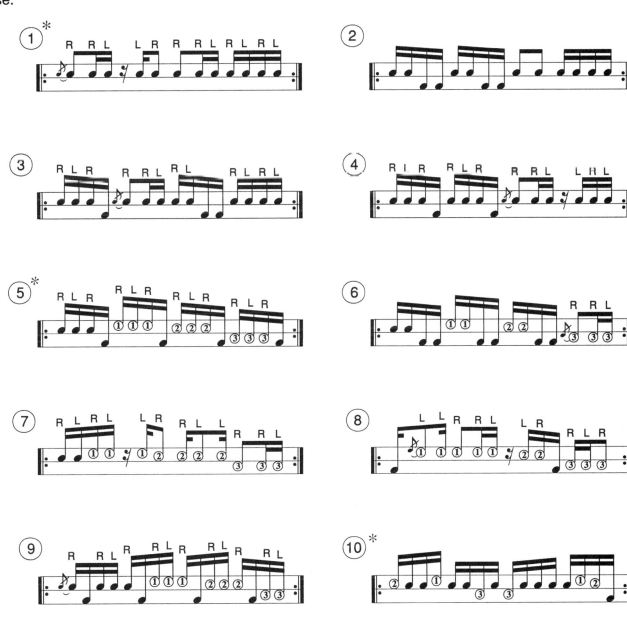

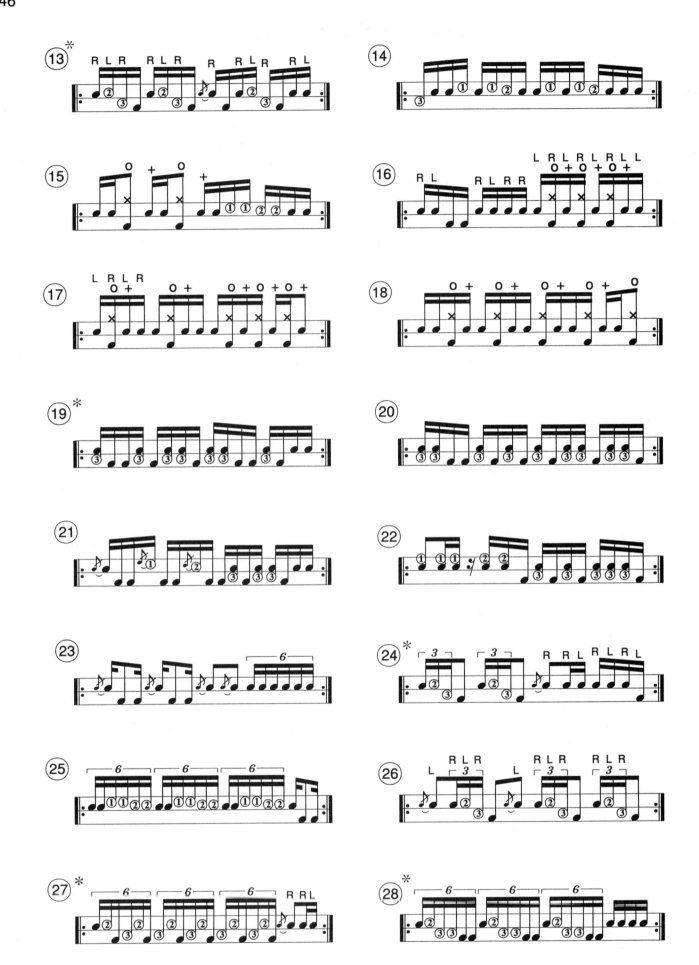

For even more one-bar fills, try combining any of the preceding two-beat ideas together.

SECTION III: THE RIFF WORKSHOP

Now that we have a complete arsenal of killer groove and fill ideas, let's make some music! The purpose of the riff workshop is to provide you with a variety of musical excerpts or themes that you can play along with, offering practical application of some of the material we've covered in this book. On the accompanying recording, you'll find the following patterns corresponding by number with each of the ten different riffs. This format includes music and click track minus the drums. Note that while each of these patterns are "custom-tailored" for each riff, you may also feel free to experiment with some alternative groove ideas. Either way, make sure you stay with the click and play with "the band." Once you get comfortable with a particular example, try throwing in a few two-beat and/or one-beat fills at the appropriate time, (the end of a 4 or 8 bar phrase). Concentrate on a smooth and steady transition between the pattern and the fills and...

MAKE IT GROOVE!

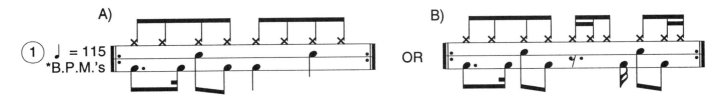

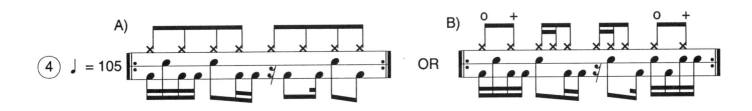

* = Beats Per Minute

EL03821

48

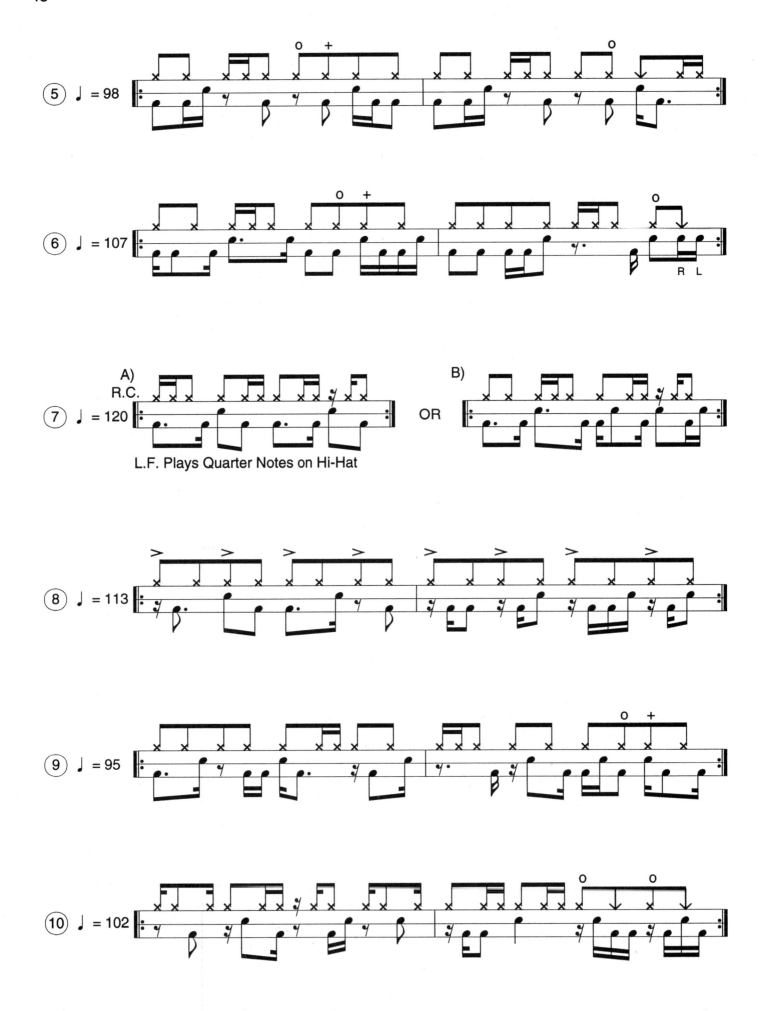

EL03821